Berlin Fresco

Also by Norbert Hummelt

Poetry
knackige codes (1991)
singtrieb (1997)
Zeichen im Schnee (2001)
Stille Quellen (2004)
Totentanz (2007)

Prose
Wie Gedichte entstehen (with Klaus Siblewski, 2009)

Translations
T.S. Eliot: Das öde Land / The Waste Land

as Editor
W.B. Yeats: Die Gedichte (2005)
Quellenkunde: Gedichte

Norbert Hummelt

Berlin Fresco
Selected Poems

Translated and introduced by
Catherine Hales

Shearsman Books
Exeter

First published in the United Kingdom in 2010 by
Shearsman Books Ltd
58 Velwell Road
Exeter EX4 4LD

www.shearsman.com

ISBN 978-1-84861-096-5
First Edition

Original poems copyright © 1997, Urs Engeler Editor;
copyright © 2001, 2004, 2007, Luchterhand Literaturverlag GmbH, München.
Uncollected poems copyright © 2009, 2010, Norbert Hummelt.
Translations copyright © 2010, Catherine Hales.

The right of Norbert Hummelt to be identified as the author of this work has been asserted by him in accordance with the Copyrights, Designs and Patents Act of 1988, and the right of Catherine Hales to be identified as the translator thereof has likewise been so asserted.
All rights reserved.

Acknowledgements
We would like to thank to Luchterhand Literaturverlag GmbH and to Urs Engeler Editor for their kind permission to publish these translations.
The poems translated here first appeared in the following original collections: *singtrieb* (Engeler, 1997), *Zeichen im Schnee* (Luchterhand, 2001), *Stille Quellen* (Luchterhand, 2004) and *Totentanz* (Luchterhand, 2007). The original uncollected poems 'deutscher herbst' and 'vorfrühling' appeared in *Jahrbuch der Lyrik 2009*, ed. Christoph Buchwald and Uljana Wolf
(S. Fischer Verlag, Frankfurt am Main 2009).

Some of these translations previously appeared in the following magazines:
*The Atlanta Review, Great Works, Horizon Review, No Man's Land,
Poetry Salzburg Review, Shearsman, Tears in the Fence,*
and online at www.lyrikline.org.

Contents

Introduction   9

dimmed light
- dimmed light   17
- trip   18
- cut   19
- haze   20
- portrait   21
- dead things   22
- from far away   23
- winter journey   24

signs in the snow
- relic   27
- codes   28
- first snow   29
- sonnet with morpheus   30
- déjà vu   31
- night   32
- under the bell jar   33
- against the light   34
- movie   35
- the signs in the snow   36
- fruit. verse narrative   37

silent sources
- turner, death on a pale horse   49
- dürer's young venetian girl   50
- the song of the black letter   52
- ice floes   53
- traces   54
- alchemy   55
- trance   56
- vigil   57
- silent sources   58
- after image   59

dance of death

blues	63
dance of death	64
berlin fresco	65
memling's madonna	66
constable	67
exit	68
valleys	69
meander	70
september light	71
from the depths	72
night song	73
rooms	74
calendar	75
antiphon	76
all hallows	77
legend	78
underground	80
tobernalt	82
primrose street	83
crossing	84

pan's hour — uncollected poems

etching	87
early spring	88
indian summer	89
german autumn	90
pan's hour	91
syrinx	92
fire	93
the year of the soul	94
ferns	95

Author's Notes   97

Berlin Fresco

An Introduction to the
Selected Poems of Norbert Hummelt

Norbert Hummelt's poems engage with the present—a present that is so deeply immersed and rooted in the past as to be almost indistinguishable from it. They are permeated with the memory of places and spaces once inhabited, dense with the remembered landscapes of his childhood, even when the specific landscape in which the poems take place are those of the present. Past and present landscapes blend and merge, the one is inextricably part of the other.

Hummelt was born in 1962 in Neuss in the Rhineland and lived there and in Cologne until moving to Berlin in 2006. Distance in space and time allows him to stand back and see better. Distinctively Rhineland landscapes are overlaid in part by those of the rural Brandenburg that has become a vital part of his life in Berlin; though the latter is not dissimilar to that of the Lower Rhineland, albeit less populated, and can call up layers of memory from that other world of his childhood and merge with them; as he writes in the poem 'ferns': ". . . images from earlier blended in I do not know what / level of memory engendered them . . ." Again, in the same poem, electricity pylons straddle the Brandenburg landscape as they did in the remembered Rhineland one, and seem like part of the landscape because of that association, seem to be a fact of nature, with no apparent connection to the light that comes on at the touch of a switch.

As the title of one of his collections, *Silent Sources*, hints, sources are important to the poet, in two main areas: his own life, and written texts that are available as sources. "What direction is poetry going in today?" he has asked, and supplied the answer, "To the sources!" Sources as origin, but also, as for the salmon, as the place to which we need to return to get new life.

Thus, the myths and legends associated with the Rhineland landscape, too, provide material, in a manner reminiscent of Stefan George, as in 'legend'. The external facts of landscapes and their objects and legends are transformed by the musicality and rhythm of his lines into internal landscapes with their overlapping strata of time, thus making the poems into places of introspection as well as looking outwards; and it is this very internalisation, and this strong sense of place, that make Norbert Hummelt's poems instantly recognisable and make him almost unique in contemporary German poetry.

Inseparable from the landscape of the Lower Rhine around Neuss as a fixed point in and source of Hummelt's poetry is his family. The Lower Rhineland is the place where he learned to speak and see, and so it has left the mark of the mother tongue on him, the language which is vital for a poet. His father died when he was young, so his defining memories of him are also childhood memories, such as that recounted in 'movie', of walks through that Rhineland landscape, of places seen with his father, such as we see in the poem 'crossing', and for ever intimately connected in those memory levels with him. Since his mother's death recently, as he has said in a radio talk, he no longer has anyone he can ask to check the veracity of his memories; thus, poetry is a way of retrieving and ordering memory, but, at the same time the poems are a way of bringing his parents within calling distance. The poem is unthinkable without the fact of mortality, without their living and dying.

Another early childhood and early language experience which is important for an understanding of Hummelt's poetry is the mystery of the ritual of the Latin Mass, which has become part of the structure of his language: "It was I think in the long silences during the Mass that I found the correlation between elevated form and interruptive sounds as a pattern that is fundamental to my poems, for these silences were broken by sounds made by my mother, which she was unable to suppress, and which I would now recognise anywhere."

The poems, then, are often strongly autobiographical, and the first-person narrator is Hummelt himself; dispensing with any post-modern games, this is an imaginative recreation of memory. Often, it is art that enables him to access those memories; sometimes, as in 'dürer's young venetian girl', the picture itself is evoked as a memory, that used to hang on the wall in the living room of his childhood home and, similarly to Proust's madeleine cake, allows him to recreate the discomfort of a tumescent boy amid the claustrophobia of "schnapps and sandwiches" and neighbourhood gossip; or, as in 'memling's madonna', finding a cheap print of the painting of the title by the 15th Century Flemish artist Hans Memling while clearing out his cellar permits him to demystify that past. Then again, memory of parties and dancing can be triggered by the fall of light through windows of empty rooms about to be deserted ('blues') or driving along the autobahn past the turn-off to a barn where there were once all-night parties to keep the fear of the dark at bay ('dance of death'); elsewhere a moment of regret for a lost past can be inferred between the lines from the derelict state of a house in the present ('rooms').

His father is a strong presence in the poems by his absence. Not only his father, but also other family members form points of reference and grounding for the imaginative world of the poems. In 'dimmed light', the darkened room is remembered where his grandmother lay with festering bedsores; in 'silent sources', his uncle hovers between life and death while Hummelt seeks solace in the "silent sources" of memories of times shared with him, of water, bars and the Catholic mass. In 'crossing' Hummelt remembers walks with his father in the area near their home, and the small stream marking the boundary between Aachen and Cologne becomes a kind of Styx without the ferryman; you can cross it in a single step—death is that close.

The section titles of the volumes *Silent Sources* ('silent sources', 'rhine province', 'legends', and 'distant thunder') and *Dance of Death* ('the silent house', 'dream novella', 'berlin fresco' and 'world news') are eloquent guides to Hummelt's exploration of his main themes and concerns.

More recently the landscape has widened to include (and transform!) other places—Ireland, New York, London. In 'tobernalt', visiting the Holy Well in the place of that name in Sligo, Ireland, leads into an almost mystic vision of the scene during the Penal Times in the 17th and 18th Centuries, which becomes entwined with the present; while 'primrose street' evokes a feeling of dislocation in a strange place with strange people who speak a strange tongue that "must be irish", and the poet is trapped in a cave in a "mountain of dull sound"; Manhattan's Fifth avenue and the pillars of the Brooklyn Bridge are steep gullies ('valleys'); while going down into the London Underground evokes a vision of people sheltering there during the Blitz of World War II and of caves with mystic spiral carvings and the building of Stonehenge, with allusions to Eliot's 'Four Quartets' ('underground'). Berlin gets a mention as well, with the discovery of a medieval frieze in the Marienkirche near Alexanderplatz in 'berlin fresco' and a contemplation of the distant past of the last ice age, when Greifswalder Strasse, where Hummelt lives, was a melt-water gully feeding the Urstromtal ('meander'). The present feels like no more than a thin layer of dust covering an overpowering past. Journeys can be dislocations ('codes') between past and present lives and landscapes of childhood and adulthood tenuously connected by the telephone ('calendar'). The night is a site of potential terror ('night', 'night song') while dreams take over consciousness ('trance') or become mystical visions as in 'antiphon' or 'exit', or, as in 'from the depths', fragments emerge into—and merge with—daytime experience. Just as art is often the trigger for memory, so too is it often a point of access to those dream or trance-like states; in 'etching', the narrator falls asleep over an etching by the Dutch artist Hercules Seghers and is drawn into the landscape depicted there, waking up just as it is becoming all too real.

Interestingly, the art referenced is mostly German or Flemish/Dutch work from the 15th to 19th Centuries, as well as English landscape painters, especially Constable and Turner. The effect of this is to contribute to a feeling of pre-modern, or at least pre-20th Century, stasis in the poems. This complements the language of the poems, which is redolent with frequent allusions to and echoes of such classic German writers as Adalbert Stifter, Stefan George and Friedrich Hölderlin, whose cadences are unmistakable and layered into the poems, frequently by way of quotations.

Hummelt's way of working within and out of the tradition is quite different from, for example, that of Thomas Kling, another Rhinelander. Kling is more like an archaeologist, excavating and refashioning language; he has been very influential for the younger generation of poets in Germany. Hummelt has taken a different path, so it is interesting that it is precisely Norbert Hummelt who has edited Kling's *Selected Poems*. One is also reminded of that great, and sadly late, writer W.G. Sebald, who deliberately used a more classical frame of language, frequently echoing Stifter and others, in rejection of the language and culture of the post-war Germany he despised. For Hummelt, however, the past is ever present in the present which is unthinkable without it and his language reflects this. In Hummelt's poem 'indian summer', both poem and title recall Stifter's novel of the same name (in German, *Nachsommer*); the poem describes a retreat, albeit temporary, from the modern day by avoiding a traffic jam to set off across country to a place remembered from an earlier summer; while the section title 'dream novella' from *Dance of Death* is taken straight from the Arthur Schnitzler novella *Traumnovelle* (which was also the basis of Kubrick's film, *Eyes Wide Shut*). Hummelt, does, however, also take on board—and is influenced by—such classic Modernists as Gottfried Benn and T.S. Eliot.

As well as six collections of poetry, including three from Luchterhand, part of Random House (*Signs in the Snow*, 2001, *Silent Sources*, 2004, and *Dance of Death*, 2007), Norbert Hummelt has also published new translations into German of Eliot's 'Four Quartets' and 'The Waste Land' and edited and co-translated an anthology of translations of W.B. Yeats. As has been noted, there are allusions to Eliot throughout the poems, and a passage from 'Four Quartets' provides the epigraph to the volume *Dance of Death*. However, the presence of such writers as Stefan George, Adalbert Stifter, Gottfried Benn, Friedrich Hölderlin, and others, reveal a durable and deep rooting in the traditions of German literature beyond contemporary fashion that we also glimpse in Kling's work. Indeed, some poems work mainly through such allusions and cannot really be translated, since they rely so heavily on knowledge of the poems being alluded to for their effect; while, on the other hand, an earlier poem (in Kling mode), 'oh, that sickly picture' (from the early collection *'knackige codes'* (*crispy codes*, 1993), does not necessarily need us to know the Benn original ('Oh, that Distant Land') it parodies for us to enjoy it.

Norbert Hummelt's use of rhyme and assonance is a conspicuous feature of his poetry. However, he sees these 'internal rhymes' (often slant rhymes) as end rhymes that just don't happen to be at the end of lines, rather at the end of (irregular) rhythmic and syntactic units that run freely beyond line-breaks. This is what gives the poems much of their individual musicality and heightens the effect of internal landscaping. More important for him than line breaks is the form of the poem on the page, lines of more or less equal length appearing as a block. The translations follow this principle, so that the lines and line breaks of the German and English texts do not often correspond. The 'internal rhymes' and assonances of the English versions are not those of the original. The aim has been to create poems that work in English and give an English-speaking reader a feel for the musicality of the original, but on their own terms. Likewise, Hummelt's trademark use of the abbreviated form "u." instead of "und" cannot be reproduced by "a." for "and", since the abbreviation, while common in German usage, would be exotic in English, as would the ampersand, which, though often used in poetry, is not in common usage; "and" is used throughout.

But perhaps it would be better to use the word *adaptation* rather than *translation*; since, as Robert Frost observed, the first thing that gets lost in translation is the poetry, it is incumbent upon the "translator" to "adapt" the poem into the medium of a different language and, of course, make it function there, with all its "strangeness", while keeping as much as possible of the feel of the original. At the same time, translation is also a collaboration—between the original author and the translator, or should we say: adaptor, since the original will always be a part of and a frame of reference for the adaptation that results. It is a lucky adaptor who has the enthusiastic, active and positive cooperation of the original poet, as this adaptor has had with Norbert Hummelt, and she wishes to thank him for this collaboration.

Catherine Hales
Berlin, July 2009

dimmed light

dimmed light

pavement already shut down
disconcerted in the mist of a
winter evening, one more time
around the same block with
its blacked-out thickly-curtained
facades; where you are heading
dimmed light, calendar pages
long since no longer torn off *give
the lad some cherry juice* in
a simple glass, slopped and
bunkered the things we're
conscious of *and give him
something from the sweet tin
too* some of those chocolate
twists two wrapped in gold paper
as were the open legs, raw with
bedsores in this room here brace
yourself as the images come to you

trip

somewhere between drifting and
dreaming my hand in your hair
stroking mechanically now
what images are with you as you slip
into sleep .. nothing
taken not on a trip
just pin-pricks surrounding
your iris perhaps a bit
like the way a bird in flight
is no longer able to alight
on a branch that's been sawn off
my arm beneath you is getting
heavy my hand
is numb and in my head
the pirate copies in the other eye
are more fleeting still than photography

cut

with the discrete images in the room
from a dream he'll never tell
he moves into the dull
hallway light the silent object wrapped
in parchment
and with the transient idea of blood
on his chin concealed with a little
printer's ink he kicks numbly into
the too-bright morning far below
foam rubber *when I'm dead*
and gone to his friend in a shoebox
small roses going cold.
the small pit beneath the balcony

haze

you seek the nearness of what's
outlived and why ever not? no-one's
looking after all as you press down the
handle on the door and even the man
eating green beans from a flask is hardly
taking any notice you've taken down a slim
volume from the shelf: the letters clinging
still to words the dedication gone, the
language's fruit pulp smelling so sweetly
of decay your jacket's elbows worn to holes
and the man who wore it before you not long
passed away. it's all the same. sometimes
though you'd go although still young and
take refuge in your local pub with its tinted
windows blocking any view of impending
dusk smoky air and lips hidden in the haze
of someone else's words that don't mean you.
is the century not over yet? you sit with a
plate of egg and chips reading t.s. eliot
in one of those old faber paperbacks

portrait

ash-blonde wind-blown and ousted
from the world
what's left of things already just
forgetting, rote reciting
sitting eating the last of gherkins
flickering, eye almost fluttering even
a tic perhaps too much alone
in her caravette / in rhyming speech
to herself and for the
rest of the trip
hear her song drift from a fastened
sphere, to nobody visibly
who was supposed to hear
the dialogue of dress and stitch.

dead things

in the sleepy wake of a
day in april
there's the same tormented pigeon
the empty drink can shoved
into a bush, the yoghurt tub
between branch and twig
which itself is stuck and that
since last winter things seemingly
left unchanged as though
they'd merely been photographed
thus flees the precisely-found image
into memory, *where otherwise safe
in the dark* of evening at the edge
of the road in low grass steeped
in long-distance light terrified
the rabbit *my eye the thorn* fro-
zen in its movement in the mo-
ment its vulnerable body / the
shadow of a blackbird flits
silently overhead and van-
ishes into a wall of forsythias

from far away

amid dark ivy, in the driveway
to the company yard, they're in the weathered wall
from there a vision came to me
of the cries of starlings and yet they are
not visible a twitching in my
scribbling hand .. I do not know
whether they're only staying for the winter
perhaps or are they here for longer .. those
from far away *debating weighty matters*
what clouds of them on the arm of the crane
rose up at a secret signal
and turned inwards
towards the wall .. how did the birds
conceive of this idea .. what systems
guide their flight .. never
quite the same and unrepeatable
adrift in emptiness like my name

winter journey

what I have read I have read. *I search in vain in the snow
for the trail of her shoes*, narcissus search in this
artificial winter, or winter journey as an inventory to use:
my language, my eye, my window, my square.
in daytime in nighttime it pulls me outside, something
about the eyes it draws me outside, it pulls me out on to
the square, the bright reflection, *beautiful seeing*; with eyes
with ears, crossing places, crossing time / but how
is winter supposed to arrive if it's never really
night here, I read in the paper that winter will be
nothing more than a quotation this year / the colour of night,
the colour of winter, but when I look out into the street
everything stays the same; the colours of traffic lights in white
neon light, a snow arc light in this artificial winter,
blossoming of trees in late february / a climatic shift,
it's called, a shifting in time, it's called, a
shifting of words, crossing places, crossing time / where
can I find someone now who will lend me a language,
nothing can be heard, *and when the snow falls at the window*,
what then, what happens then to my blossoming words,
the rosebuds, japanese cherry, *and where when it's winter
shall I find* the bright shining gleam of the street? outside
in the square the traffic lights have gone out, total
exhaustion of all sources of light; there is no *lily* there,
there is no *cup*, it's a *winter journey* from you to yourself:
actually these were meant you say as lines for a poem that didn't
make it into the world, the word snowcheeks would weigh
too heavily / as only floating they were able to carry each
other a wind game played by two winter feathers, a stirring
of snowflakes / the snow falling you say more densely with every
word, the snow settling you say on every word, language of snow,
white field of words, her face you say turned so very white.
not here. not now. we lay awake for as long as time took.
for mill-wheels are racing in every sparkling brook

signs in the snow

relic

just this bit of wall still already gone over
blackened by the rubbing of my finger–
tip as in the dark I was looking for the

crucifix, here where the carpet is almost
through, you see, and couldn't get to sleep
before I'd found it: the bronze relief, the

group of figures, I stroked across it,
was absorbed by it and heard its soft
metallic approval and so was able to

await the dreams, the dreams. this is
how the light felt in the darkness
a smeared section in a picture ..

codes

even more cryptic
since this journey began
first the book sank into your lap
then it slipped completely
from your lax grip
the letters came away
from their white background, shimmered
and went out.
you the passenger arriving are
not the same as the one who
boarded the train without looking up
you dozed off briefly
not light, not darkness
the small dissolution in your head
after the first cigarette
your closed eye has
already wandered a little on ahead
each barcode
giving you a strange look

first snow

you say you already knew as you walked
to the window it's the blackbird eyeing us there
as deeply as you lying in my arms it held

itself tightly to itself in flight and now it's sitting
silently where in the dark fork yet another
trace of something white remains that must surely

just have come overnight and drifts down like dust
when it lifts from the branch you say in your sleep
you've smelled the first snow although

we have not yet spoken of what separates us
will the rowan berries not yet soon be frozen
I've just seen their glow in the filigree of branches

sonnet with morpheus

at first the air is sweet with soft intoxication
as we eat this cake our eyelids snap shut one by one
then the world bends inwards in its dislocation
but in our breast only this silent beat goes on

this is music to send me nodding off
and all I can see then is this grass
I'm getting weary of seeing things like van gogh
the almond cutting is flowering white in the cloudy water glass

what pictures then. I slipped under and succumbed
to hesitate between holding on and letting go
then the cake is gone, we've eaten every crumb

and all thought sinks and I am strangely warm
how is it possible that I can touch you now
you are suddenly so far away encircled in my arm

déjà vu

just don't take your hand away from my hair
and do keep on stroking my trembling scalp
be still. be calm. do it. don't stop.
how the pattern on this floor disturbs me.
tell me something, anything, just talk to me.
here is a cluster of moments of panic
what I could visualise has now imploded
and is returning endlessly expanded into time
here is that record that's always jumping
you know and don't know the fucking song
you can't escape your own skin, the space in your head
and each beat of an eyelash is an abomination
and each sentence someone speaks a shock and a blow
and each word has gravity and weight
and drags me down, image do not strike me dead
just don't take your hand away from my hair
and do keep on stroking my trembling scalp
be still. be calm. do it. don't stop.

night

just switch off the lamp when you come back from
the toilet let's sleep for even the neon light over
there is taking its light back: its rather unhealthy
green shimmer will stay switched off for the rest
of the night. from now on there will only be paleness
here in our room, mercury dreams, body temperature
hitting the floor, I think there's something wrong with
my armpit. we merely guess at what is happening
beneath us, quite noiselessly flesh for fantasy; only
sometimes, by day, do you recognise washing stands,
if one of the windows is open, for as long as it's being
aired. under the crack of the door a smell is coming now
I was just thinking of turpentine, you know that too,
that's a childhood word. for in the night when I couldn't
sleep (I was afraid of the completely white eyes of
the apocalyptic sect in that science fiction film) I lay
there alone and listened, listened, the key turning,
turning but not yet in the lock, only a car that was
passing pushing its silent headlight through the crack
in the curtains so that it swept along the wall and made
a pattern on the ceiling. and from the stairs a smell
of turpentine. we know little and notice nothing; only
like the blackbird sometimes beneath the container
maybe looking for leftovers it seems familiar when I'm
hungry. you've turned over; now I'm wide awake again
and can see the dream fluttering in your eye.

under the bell jar

the magnolias are still not
yet at their zenith however
something's pressing my left
eyelid and sending shockwaves
to my brain as though the lilac
had already passed me by

hold the bell jar up it's not
yet time to lower it again, for god's
sake please, not around me all I
want is to keep breathing so
that I can get enough air, artificially
dilate my pupils with eyedrops

so that just this once I do not
miss their blooming, the white
flashes of the chestnut trees
of which I'll dream in this
capsule now and for ever more
with all my veins and arteries

against the light

on the sixth day before the end of january in the
morning light bevelled with winter at the edge of the
island between track and track in the garbage *beneath
the bushes sat an earnest bird
songless*, it spoke alone as I stood close beside it for
maybe the duration of an entire cycle of the traffic lights
"in vain you try to describe your day in words nothing
very much can be said about those images that are quite
distressing and really rather sloppy and the occasional
appetite perhaps you can wish yourself very far from here
if you look hard and long and completely surrender
yourself the world of things begins to bend to your
gaze and shows you everything you secretly love
it may be the top of a gasometer the silhouette of
a distant mountain .. now go and see if you can find
something to help you do that because you cannot
bear very much reality" and its voice sank and echoed
and faded in the dense crowd of the other voices in
the underground and slipped down below to where
we were all going, the floating escalator beneath our feet ..

movie

in the first twilight this side of the curtain
even before supper, the black-and-white
programme running, I would sit, a child,
leaning against his knees, and his hand
would softly stroke my head. but hours later,
when in *der kommissar* or in the movie
from the *usa* a lady rather sparsely dressed
or a couple too closely entangled could be
seen his hand would slide over my eyes
and stay until the scene was over, my
heart pounding while I was in the dark.
only the sound remained, a groaning or
sighing, since remote control had not
yet been invented, so that an image came
of its own accord into my mind and with it
desires and my first embarrassment.

the signs in the snow

willow catkins swinging in the wind, though
not yet imaginable as buds as long as it's
december and the physical world in doubt
*funny that fixed itself in my mind because
it was so real* amid the still-falling snow we'd
be walking until I can see nothing more
on the endlessly snowed-over planks in a
photo that's exposed over and over .. my
eyes are held though so that I cannot distinguish
the wish from the wish, hardly sure of the
figures standing before me in winter parkas
fastened up to the neck nor of the mourning
edge around the black-and-white photos, for
ever shivering under my anorak .. you can
only ever see two people in photos because
one has to press the shutter, as though the body
of the missing third person *forgive me I was
sixteen* were already sunken in the silent moor,
long ago layered over by bodies of complete
strangers, turned to peat and undecayed, yet
one being with the cotton grass, reeds and rushes.

fruit. verse narrative

I

morello cherries, sugared, destoned, and
peach halves, so called from the way they
tasted half of tin and half of peach

and mirabelle plums conserved in jars
but still retaining their stones from which
your tongue hesitantly separates the thin

scraps of flesh, tenderly hurting itself
such is the memory that fills my mouth
a hint of dessert, once overpowering

the more rustic aroma of mettwurst, butter
beans and sauerkraut with the corners
of my mouth cracked, scabbed in winter

(the mustard from düsseldorf hot with such a bite)
before lunch, so digestible, culminated
in ritual .. you know, the syllables were

so heavily slurred, a familiar droning sound, so
that it took years for the words to take on
their individual meanings and disentangle from

their mysterious wreath. but I can still hear
their patterning, certain sounds we were
aware of at an early age, like those from the

single record with the star label, music in the style
of early fifties hits to which my sister, according to
reports, jigged like crazy in her baby chair

but you never heard it .. certain sounds we were
aware of at an early age, and they're probably the
last thing that remains in us when we cannot even

talk to ourselves any more. so much for the manner
of a melodrama; my sister had no idea what she was
nodding to. only our mother knew the secret sounds

surrounding the experience of birth with a first
symphony by brahms: in the maternity ward
was a radio .. perhaps nordmende or

telefunken, I still know that myself, the crackling,
hissing, song of the sirens I could pick up
when the dial would turn no further.

modulating noise at the extreme edge of the trans-
mission range, west of lahti, rias, hilversum ..
those were names belonging just to me, without

the accompaniment of spoken words, just written
signs, when on days in bed with a fever everything
slowed down, gazing again and again into the

magical lidless eye, the way it widened,
blinked and closed, and I, making it happen, sat
in awe of it with mirabelles from the said preserving jar.

II

on a day like this in bed with a fever, at some time
or other even the voice in the room didn't seem to mean
me any more, the words apparently dissolving

into kitchen haze and slipping unrecognised
to the cool crack of the window. I was the one waiting
and holding the towel and silently taking receipt

of those moist things, so absorbed in them as to be
able to count them all off as they constantly slipped
through my fingers: the small spoons

kept multiplying (used for ersatz coffee
or fruit dessert), while the stirrer,
saw-edged knife, cake-slice stayed topped

with foam on the draining board .. and so
the afternoon arrived with apple turnovers,
the time of youth seemed not to be too willing

to disappear just yet, except on the torn-off leaves
of the calendar, in the whirring sound of fast forward
and rewind of a cassette with a recording of

the latest top of the pops (done without a cable
with the built-in microphone) the passing of
its moments was tangible, but that

was play: tripping off the tongue as lightly
as the melody of our pet canary singing completely
without reason not even in reply to the twittering

of a blackbird coming in through the kitchen window ..
and in the depths of a sunday evening
at the still point of the turning world

I press stop and turn over the cassette
and switch the recorder on again:
first a rustling, half-smothered words

somebody coughing whom I don't recognise
something being poured out, but not too much
then the reply, a little attack of laughing

a jumble of voices, a noticeable crackling
(I think the wafer rolls were right next to
the microphone) and then a toast, sup-

pressed giggling, a clink of glasses, but
I never hear it: the last take with the
familiar voice, imprisoned here on this unreal

ribbon, very soon it started stretching
and vanished into the cupboard for fear
of a tangle of tape and of hearing it again

here is the box, a band's songs are still
written on it in a child's hand,
the name rainbow with a multi-coloured pen.

III

certain images that we could never understand
like that poster, vaguely remembered
a young man's long unruly hair as he

put an object he desired to his lips
and it looked as though
a soft ice cream (chocolate marshmallow)

was going up in smoke and flames .. hung on
the end wall of the forbidden room, the store
room where his sisters slept, which his parents

could not understand, nobody talked about it
perhaps the inner sleeve of a long-playing
record or icon of awaked desire to be

close to the stars that shone in through the
opening, if they could be seen deep and un-
conscious and even more weightless than

the other images that came and went,
came again and again and stayed without trace
in the furnished room. the late news flits by

like a phantom. and now and again a bit
of news heard again that was recorded then
but not really understood, like this one:

baader is permitted to play ping pong, but why ever
wouldn't he be? I searched all the reference books I
knew but the reason for the why not just eluded me

and I read the *bader* catalogue a lot: it was on
the corner seat where nobody sat next to
neckermann and not far from *quelle* mail order

inconspicuous in a pile of newspapers *battles*
continuing for the old imperial city ..
it was the way it was put that sounded so

familiar that the world's events seemed
to touch me softly and I thought aachen
was in vietnam .. as clear as the way friday

stood for ever in the sign of the fish
finger in the cycle of weeks and in the sway
too of rice pudding with cinnamon

and with sugar and plums, plums in borrowed
juice, in fact the sealing rings on the preserving
jars have long since been completely useless,

when all eyes as they say are waiting for
you, why have you still not come back, is your
briefcase not still in its place, there

leaning against the leg of the sofa (I never look)
with sandwiches and refreshing wipes
as though packed for a long car journey.

IV

I dream loose chippings I dream ground plates
my scalp puckers, vibrates as I dream
with the soft and constant thudding against

glass, glass, then there is a jolt to my head I
surface slowly: is the motorway lit up all night
here? no, we're just passing a ghost town

cooling towers, warehouses, pipes, smoke, everything
glowing in the white light that nearly blinds me,
sunken again, are we nearly there? when is it

finally going to get light? will there be another traffic
jam on the ahr valley bridge? the sort of questions that
a child will ask. it's not yet certain where the journey will end.

everything still happens as though it's the first time round
and yet every half-remembered tree, blurred slope, distant
view and tank gauge blinks brightly anticipating our return.

that's the joy of anticipation that can't be suppressed
when the looked-forward-to signpost first appears: just
1 km more, the indicator's on, you haven't even started

to eat your sandwich. but as soon as that same
afternoon, when we leave the village for our first
walk through the orchards, the fields here haven't

been mown yet, poppies, cornflowers, nobody is watching
as I run to the edge of the woods where the ferns
are waist high, the trampled paths have all grown over

and by evening I have a stone in my shoe, night
is dark in this pension but not quite silent
even though the sounds of the animals in the stables

next door can hardly be heard at all, the rattling chain
of the dead farm dog, the prowling of cats across the barn roof
intruded on by only the rise and fall of voices in the pub

which entice me downstairs, already in my pyjamas, already
on the stairs, on tiptoe, feeling my way down, through
the light in the crack of the door I can recognise them all

louder than life, I want to knock, but I do not dare,
surrounded as I am now by a certain mix of scents, so
that I pause now on the silent threshold: it is not hay, not

straw, nor anything like what's usually known as country air.
it's the smell of beer and beeswax, blue toilet cleaning blocks,
completely different from how I know them, yes, even vomit

is in there somewhere, in the cool movement of the air
the night brings us, secretly mingled with just a little forest.
this is the joy that always sings in me. here on the

postcard showing the bar the sunbathing meadow
and the village avenue I can walk down the path right
to the mill. on this card the village is empty, still.

V

the unconscious way of the regular issue chocolate
bar, a packet of semolina pudding that's past its
use-by date, lets me see the hollow in

his pale calf where a bullet was
that suddenly hits me. just the sort of stories
that we've long forgotten, hardly glancing

at the writing, faded sütterlin: the up
and downstrokes of his signature I tried
to imitate as a child, what he thought, felt,

is not there in the words, just some set phrase
is all his son receives and makes the creases
in the foreign forehead all his own, the rest is pure

projection. but what happens in the evenings when
you go out and meet a girlfriend and I
lie here alone until you come home and stars,

here there are no stars to be seen again and when
perhaps I'm looking out of this window now, out
at the street where the sounds are, again I can see

nothing but bright advertising hoardings but
at the moment when I close my eyes
the universe is here, dark blue, deep. the verse

acts as though no time has passed, at least
I feel as I am telling it the suspicion of a
presence, just last night I had hardly

dropped off to sleep, the brimstone butterfly
sitting lightly on my shoulder, seeming to me
so ghostly yet so real and we were deep

in conversation as though nothing were more
natural, standing in tall unmowed grass
on the fenced-in meadow at the far

end of the garden, until a woman's voice
called down from the balcony
startling me up as your mouth

was kissing me; it's only half-past
midnight, you've come home, I'm burning
up, here feel my forehead .. I sprinkle

reichenhaller bath salts into my foot
bath because, as I learned early on,
that's the brand that draws the cold

out of the body, just as grapefruit juice
is supposed to reduce blood pressure. it's
the aftertaste that gifts the memory

certain fruits we ate as children
grated apple, raspberry syrup
redcurrants on a foam of beaten cream.

silent sources

turner, death on a pale horse

yes, at the end he was only painting light
yet this does not explain the lack of light
the half rump the way it lies in shadow
the way the skeleton is balanced
across the withers the arm the hand all bone
stretched out forwards crossing the pale
neck of the beast the way it rises & shies
straining its nostrils into the darkness ridden
by one who knows its back high away
from the glistening path from the heat ever on
pulverised to light until the varnish burns

dürer's young venetian girl

with the strawberry blonde corkscrew curls, the black
ribbon on her left shoulder, necklace, lips, perfect
complexion, her brown eyes looking inwards

hung over the television or just next to that where the
sideboard was and the chaise longue, near the view
of münster and the calendar *beautiful sauerland* .. and yet

pictures were hardly ever talked about, and if then that
painting of a battle that looked so exotic in the dark
hallway and on it the sentence: *the germans to the front*

only no eyes looking inwards. nobody came late:
a schnapps a sandwich, occasionally there was a smell
of gas and a ring dove calling in the courtyard

pictures were only mentioned at the edge of conversations
and hardly ever ruisdael's *windmill near wijk* with a coastal
landscape beneath heavy clouds, in which in one place

the waves are crinkling the water but there's no wind to stretch
the canvas of the sails: we weren't told about such fine details
in space and time, not in art and not in the real world either

and no eyes looking inwards, only juice and streusel cake
and the silent time in the soft armchair among sofa cushions
not a word about lips or corkscrew curls, and *complexion*

didn't even enter the vocabulary. instead the neighbours and all
their many and varied illnesses and someone else has died
in the old people's home, nobody came late: a schnapps a sandwich

now at last the light was on in the room, the level rose the
war the elections for the state parliament, almost nobody paying
any attention to the flickering in the background the young ice

skater from canada and in his cheeks becoming rather warm
the evidence very clearly visible of what the boy was thinking
who was behaving strangely in the armchair and staring at the

motionless pictures .. lips nameless, the throat, the necklace
the time is not long past when I lived in the erroneous belief
that she was the woman from the five mark banknote,

but then in the saturday supplement in the paper (I
read that sometimes, but not always) there she was in colour:
jewels at her throat, corkscrew curls with the corresponding

caption and the title, so that now I'm completely in
the picture: dürer's young venetian girl, whom I look at
for a little while, but her eyes simply look past me.

the song of the black letter

under the mildew spot a dragonfly's wing and
around the thread binding a spot of midge's
blood .. lord greystoke junior enters the strange
cottage scratches his nearly hairless chest
wood of the veranda creaking at every step
feels the linen or leather things and I I'm all
excited too in every fibre of my being white
as coconut milk this unknown thing is thinner
than palm leaves smooth as ivory and so many
black beetles moving on it but when he stays
still he notices that no there's not a hint not a
single stir of movement that must be the
vacillating air here in the tropics he thinks of
fever stiffness rigor mortis and sees where
initial patterns begin to form among the beetles
a similarity where the feelers wing-cases legs are
repeating is there not something already beginning
to murmur unobtrusively there lord greystoke
junior forgets the time and as he's still staring
at the beetles he hears the sounds of a strange
species his brothers and sisters cannot hear in the
tangle dark and hairy so is it his ears or my ears
in which something is singing as though of its
own accord and the compost is a termite hill and
every tossing piece of washing line the liana from
which a cry forces its way through every single
window blind into a locked and bolted apartment

ice floes

once again the ice is breaking and she tells
me again how something was dawning and
was at an end: the old stove .. the cold war ..
in my head the machine is running slowly then
all at once transformation's there: body-warm
water is beginning to flow again ice riding in floes
on the rhine we can read about this in a chronicle
the cuban crisis not long past he was only in town
in the mornings you see there wasn't so much
traffic then quiet in the crib or in his arms the one
born after his grandson listens to the sounds that
enclosed him we had only just got a telephone
and there was a stillness like the one just now
the call came as all the snow was already
thawing the earth split the way it was forty
years ago even if the fractures are not so visible
you sit in his armchair made of the old wood

traces

it's known that zebra finches can listen in their sleep to the
song of their species mates so they don't forget what it
means to be a zebra finch .. the currents of their brains

have been measured by electro-encephalograph. the young
geneaologist uses the internet, inputs more names and
extends the relationships, and one day a letter comes

from overseas, and the light blinks twice on the answering
machine but there's no message. there's only someone
breathing from a great distance comes a coughing noise,

the genetic disposition heavily lower rhine, and what's got
stuck in that throat is not easy to shift: the flat blue tin with
the white writing the dark pastilles in the shape of lozenges

you're supposed to suck in the dark night. they make your
tongue go numb so it no longer obeys your will. dreaming
has always made me completely ill: there were shadows

that were constantly moving and shifting shape a deer that fell
from the sky becoming the crash of the *challenger* becoming
a black panther that only appeared to be sleeping becoming

an image of evil, angel lucifer—what is the origin of all these
images the young genealogist uses the internet linking new
york with swidnica with andernach. some great-great uncle or

other who fell near vienna, grave among many, location unknown,
this line too died out early. what do you want with all that data
tell me: where does that tugging come from on the left side of my

chest the way I contract my scalp, why I always turn on to this side,
at a gentle angle just so that I can get to sleep I listen at night
to my eliot cassettes mouth half open amazed at being so unrelated.

alchemy

in my hand a light bulb bursts the fourth in a very
short time there was a flash in the studio over
there and above us someone's playing chopin now

it snowed for the first time on thursday I was
walking in central park and was almost blind my
head was filled with white light I didn't know

what to think there are some things that we
really cannot visualise at all and reception's
bad on this station is it because the dead

are walking among us but aren't allowed to let us
see them because it brings bad luck if it's true what
the indians say this is a place where they were killed

as the piano falls silent at the very moment when
a light bulb bursts in my hand and in my eye a small
capillary there was a flash in the studio over there

trance

distant parts begin at my rainbow skin sometimes
even here in your dark hair we kiss each other
and speak a few words I slide away and already
I'm not here .. I come to myself as we're driving in
the car I myself am steering the car stops on a
bend a spacious view we look down into a distant
world .. below in the spa they'd take stock of the
situation and every evening if the saga's true
the commander would have himself driven up to
the hilltop where looking out over hills and valleys
would make him slightly drowsy .. he gives himself
up to the deep sheen of the sun and hears from
the west where the front was an underground and
distant rumbling that he took back to the spa when
he was sleeping down there .. I wake up and feel
your hair touching a distant rumbling passing over
your forehead we kiss each other and listen in to distant
parts where a trance is ebbing away from my dark brain

vigil

long after midnight eastern time on the
spanish side of the line here in the
blocks so lost the two of us from below
something's burning or whispering to me
can't you hear it it's drifting here from
somewhere the cat is squatting by the
apartment door and speaking in foreign
tongues .. may be that someone is still there
in the corridor can't you hear it I'm sitting
here and haven't managed a single line ..
can't you hear it in my ear my blood is
pounding you were the first to see the
snow-laden sky but this hour just will not
pass until I lay back down gently beside
you and hear it: your gentle breathing

silent sources

the doctors brought him back twice, then he fell
for the third time under the high mass where he hit
the ground hard, early and in the light; in the wood

of the kneeler the small groove has long since
darkened over in the grain, only for our thoughts
a silent source where we'd sit together in later years

and cases of mineral water a constant topic with
slices cold and included in conversations which
mostly don't involve me at all. is it just coincidence

then when I wake up at night and in the hotel turn
the television on and hop channels into a documentary
near death experience, as they are calling it, isn't it

strange the way the images all agree and they always
talk about a tunnel and about a light and patients
describe how their souls fly up, but not their bodies.

I can't watch that now, not at this time of night, not
in palermo and not so alone. I ought to have a shower
and walk through the streets right down to the sea,

because day will soon be breaking; and there's sure
to be a bar open somewhere and a church where they
read mass early, silent or not, with scraps of latin.

after image

one of her early silver pictures, foil
and wire on canvas, was the first thing
of hers I saw: so shining and so empty
and laid bare on a naked wall in a

dingy bar .. in a damp and far too spacious
basement where the eye finds nothing
to fix on just her blurred and out-of-focus
photos draped on fine wires around the room

even the objects she printed in bright
colours are now dipped in a film of time
the last line was the first to come to me:
she came and went a woman in white

dance of death

blues

the light broke through the glass bricks again and
played over the tiles, the parquet, showing how yawn-
ingly empty the room was, for there was not so much
as a bed in the house. nor did it echo as it did just so
recently, which was probably because no-one was
speaking; I went slowly through the empty rooms while
the light was breaking through glass bricks. we haven't
seen these glass bricks for a long time when there was
furniture here we didn't notice them it was a winter's day
and outside the sun was shining that didn't fit into my
scheme of things I went through the empty rooms again.
then on top of that the sound of birdsong came in from
outside which I was not quite able to ignore. the light
broke through the glass bricks again I could not fail to
see it so I thought it better to go back down to the base-
ment where there was still an old mirror hanging in the
hobby room. I could see eyes in it, but they were not only
mine. there were people dancing, they were behind me.
there were peanut flips on the lino. music was playing
and a record was jumping. I turned around, but saw no-
one dancing. no flips on the floor, only dust and silence
and light pushing weakly through the basement window.

dance of death

fear of the dark is not the whole story. we hardly
know each other and don't really want much more,
the long hot summer is over and the only traffic jam
was near cologne but going in the other direction.
the barn is in the haze, the drizzle of the flat land.
it's not often that I'm the one who puts the music on.
we know each other so well and are becoming more
and more like strangers. the old score is all that stays
put in our minds. this is nothing for gentler spirits, the
racket, the posing, and the quantities of beer, but once
I found in all of this many tender wonders, and if they
came back I'd have no objection. fear of the dark leaks
from all the speakers, the lighting console can do no-
thing on its own; there's no disco ball, no dry ice. only
one song in five is still able to get our legs twitching,
but there's no more sparkle in our eyes .. if only the fog
were to come into the barn and enfold the dancing fig-
ures: in the haze, the drizzle of the flat land images are
flitting; but only the dance of the dead can be so wild.

berlin fresco

stüler is quite expecting mould as he inspects the tower
of saint mary's. they can't ventilate the nave properly: there's
a lot of damp in these old walls and it's creeping upwards.
but the plaster just here has a strange sound. the royal chief architect

taps a bit of the chalky layer off. so now they who have gone
into the still wall now come to light little by little: faces leached
of colour whitewashed over each day's area done by the fresco painter
as he applied the paint to the still-moist plaster. which has to be done

quickly for the plague is at the door: another soul captured
in stone. but death takes each one by the hand: the thin man
in his white robe the picture the crumbling script that speaks
again and again of just one thing: mr monk I would just like to say

something: see how well I can dance before you all .. god every
time I hear that I'm so sorry I still want to get this and that
finished and make it to the rhine just one more time the way it looks
in the old engravings .. and then fade for ever into the wall

memling's madonna

was completely unknown to me until I found the small
framed picture lying in the dust while I was clearing out
the cellar. a head-and-shoulders portrait, no lap, no holy

child, no angels to be seen either. you cannot see much
else apart from mary's face, eyes meditative, a small mouth,
brownish foliage as background; but I like the small

tender ear and am not averse to her light brown hair, the
dark red stola thrown over it, as worn by roman women
in the street and in the bazaar. but I have absolutely no

idea how this picture came to be in the cellar, who brought
it here and why; maybe it was no longer any use for praying
to, seemed to be dispensable with as protection in the

night, could no longer even be considered as decoration
on the wall above the sleeping child. but still the old art
shines, the cheap print stuck on a bit of wood.

constable

in some of john constable's pictures I can only
ever see clouds the way as though they could
move they hang motionless over the meadows

of salisbury. then the light falls then the mood
changes it's briefly banished beneath
the clouds: effects of light on the mood

are something I'm only too well aware of. I've been
looking at clouds half the day today the way they
were forming changing passing over white and with

threatening dark edges and was lying still as a landscape.
a few evenings ago it seemed to me as though
there was a blue cloud in the sky I called you and

wanted to show you you came outside and saw it
clearly: over the city a blanket of cloud through which
we could briefly see something else, something bright.

exit

it's not just in dream that it's often happened to
me that I've been unable to find the exit through
the right door got into trains going in the wrong
direction it was a station I only half recognised
that was a fright but I was under glass and was
fixed to that spot and could not move because
I had just got to that place in the book I began
to sense surging flushes in my blood I walked
around in the woods and could feel warm light
and slackly let myself be led to an edge images
came but they were not giving me pain any more
like they used to for beneath dead treetops the
wilderness was coming alive with fern and fox-
glove and I went back into the gullies of streets
incomprehensibly distant in my blood in its
suites of rooms without windows I walked and I
ran in circles for a while until something beneath
my jacket heaved I clutched at it with my right
hand and held it and breathed hard at the edge
of the platform I bent forward and saw the tracks

valleys

this valley as good as any in the softly carved
hollow of its trough-like form holds in its folds
some secret that disperses to nothing before

the plain in the flat land sight flees further
until it breaks on the far horizon in winter valleys
there's even more snow blocking the way if only

the slip slope sunning itself in morning light in big
cities the gullies are steeper like in manhattan
fifth avenue and like the brooklyn bridge and its

pillars which we saw close up you and I in the
depths of the one body in cracks in sofas and where
bedclothes are lying this too is a valley where here

the book is folded in the heart's rhythm on a pristine
hospital chart I have no idea myself what the cool
reason is something's always drawn me down into the ravine

meander

I read somewhere that ages ago greifswalder
strasse was one of the channels along which, when
the glaciers melted, the water made its way into
the urstromtal. the urstromtal: here they ran together,
all the channels from the city of berlin. and they
meandered merrily along and nowhere was a human
being to be seen. the water must have been quite
clear. at the very most a few animal bones floating
in it, tusk of mammoth, sabretooth, skull, elk antlers.
what a panorama it must have been if you looked
north from the tv tower. where there was otherwise
only ice, everywhere there were splits and cracks
in the floes. it had turned so unnaturally mild. the
kind of weather where you can easily catch
something. the water a torrent along greifswalder
strasse. where the tramline runs the storm howled.

september light

lake como in a misty light I've only had an hour's
sleep strange I only needed to say my name
the gates of the villa opened .. he climbed the
many steps in the garden at an age when other
people would be glad to die and came to the
edge with few words and all of them with a
rhineland colouring .. once my mother gave him
her hand and did not wash it again until the next
day after an election night he came from rhöndorf
and landed as usual at mehlem the people were
already waiting at the ferry only that my mother
would have been among them they did not know
each other personally .. she always remembered
that and would always turn the radio up louder
and bring the old man his paper and first cup of
coffee in bed every morning for he liked the idea
that someone was in power who was a year
older even than himself .. remarkable when
we talk about it now the water is sparkling
again I've only had an hour's sleep and all
around me the warm flood of september light

from the depths

today I found out that I dream colours not
just simply everything in anthracite although I did
not see any blood or glowing coals from my strangely

undermined slumber after finding no rest for
several hours and tossing and turning in bright
hunger until at last at some time I sank deeper

I did bring something up with me from way down there
just like I once you remember saw our child who's
swimming untouchably close to me in the water right

in front of me although she was only just conceived as an
image remote but clear I saw the tender may green
of young trees toned down against a dark background

night song

it's night-time again, I stand listening, bowed
over my child beside her bed, so that I can
take a breath away with me, but all is still;
her nose appears to be quite free, there's no
rattling, and it's not completely dark here in
the room, but still I can't see the rising or falling
of her cover without any doubt. everything is
uncertain in me as ever a twilight was that breaks
in through the blind. barking next door and an
ambulance are signs that the world exists. I have
to believe it, it is easy; lay thee down now and
rest, and in the dawn we'll hear the ring dove
again. its cry reminds me .. it's august, my love.
all is still. all I know for certain is that the floor-
boards creak however carefully I move. it's
happened; a brief twitch of her foot in her
sleep has touched her toy clock, it's singing;
or was it my hand stroking over the cover.
just one quick whimper so that I can go.

rooms

in this house for which I have the keys
in this apartment all the doors are ajar how-
ever often I creep across the floorboards
only half-intentionally counting the doors
I always seem to end up back at the same
place when I come back after days or weeks
something has been changed or so it seems
where I (at least I thought so) turned the
heating down everything is warm and covered
in dust and on the table there are sometimes
new notes in handwriting that I don't know in
two colours and secret signals flying to and
fro but never to me when I can't find the light
in the hallway straight away something goes
through me and I yell out loud as though
a cold gaze were grazing me from behind
and isn't it strange with all the many leads
and cables plugs and what have you leading
into the crumbling wall that tonight is actually
the first time I have ever fallen

calendar

in munich there's been a fall of snow already,
now the night concert from the *ard* .. yesterday
I quickly fell asleep listening to it. they say it's

never been so cold before on this day, my mother
says on the telephone, or anyway only in the hardest
winters, in a wavering voice to her son, outside

images blurring past: just now a vineyard slope, a
factory, a railway line, then tickets are inspected and
smoke over the forest .. and her eyes, nearly twice

as old, can see the wild plums again and their leaves
brighter than ever .. a few images have remained in the
house next door the smoke from stick incendiary bombs

then in the parlour a hint of sagrotan, things I only distantly
knew the words for. but on this day there'd never before
been snow the first to wish her happy birthday was her son.

antiphon

on leaving the town the road was blocked
but my car no longer under my control led me
on through the pitch-black morning to viewless
edges industrial areas only because I hadn't
been looking at the map had seen the signposts
always just a tick too late and couldn't find
the radio switch at the third roundabout
after a left turn there was at last something
that looked like a car-park. I locked the car
and let myself be led on through streets that
were empty at this dead hour then suddenly
a bright intuition in my breast a crack revealed
itself and something was tugging at my eye
lids until the first stripe of dawn broke though
and I could see something a kind of gate almost like
death like childhood but not like dream for three
minutes in the cool of that room the images
emerged from old stones what had been lived
exchanging itself for desires: what signs of evil
premonition had arisen around me like a strange
house turned into celebration before a pale
picture that I had not looked at for many years
and it was shaking me and would not let me go
and in the streets outside the sweetness of honey
as once more I took possession of the morning

all hallows

they haven't been locking up in the evenings for a long time now;
near the lamps you can see where you're walking because your
eyes can quickly become accustomed and gradually the whole

path appears lit up. when, if not today, can you go so late to see
your dear departed loved ones. the candles placed close to the
ground never shine so cosily and close that you could be guided

by their warm glow, even though no living person will still be about.
yet still there's one thing I don't understand. did many of the graves
not used to be covered in turf at this time of year? was I myself not

one of those who went to cover them until all the earth appeared
blanketed? now the soil has no shroud and no-one uses turf any more
these days. doesn't the ground freeze in winter any more? is there

nobody down there any more who could use a good warm blanket now
that the days (the clock has been turned back) are suddenly and rapidly
getting shorter? has the organic matter already decayed to the point

where you can hardly talk about mortal remains any more? have fungus
and bacteria finished their work? long since; but I'm not used to looking at
these things in this cool way. after all this was always the place where I

was close to the dead and within calling distance of god. there was something there that penetrated clouds. I have a three-day candle; it's almost got
light since a bird's started singing; ancestor, ancestral fear, mother and child.

legend

shortly before dawn below the castle you can see the lad feeling his
way down the slope. before him the dark shapes standing there of the
walls and turrets of the town they call oberwesel. at a time when there

were no coal barges but only rafts travelling on the river, in slow motion
and in black-and-white. according to the trier *gesta boemundi*, for which
you'll need a little latin, he was off to become a servant in the palace.

and as it came to pass, one day he was carrying a jug with soil up from
the cellar to the ground floor. that's where they must have attacked him and
there were supposed to be black-and-white photos showing the way the

blood was flowing, in gory detail. because a maid was watching through a
crack in the wall and snapped and went straight away to *boots*. as it turned
out, no film in the camera. a peasant ploughman found the corpse, according

to this source, thrown under a thorn bush, the place lay many miles from the
village. and so, it goes on, murmuring arose among the people, and this
murmuring became so loud that the people then pursued the jews, strangled,

banished, drowned or struck them down, depending on whatever was to
hand, all along the rhine and its tributaries. the hand shall bear witness,
the head shall say it. the source goes on to say that the lad was taken

forthwith to bacharach, as testified to by the chapel there, but what
a pity that no-one had a slide film to hand; so they had to rely for their
evidence on handwritten manuscripts. they would also have squeezed

his good blood out of him like wine from the press so that it could heal
the afflicted, for so it was said. but again no-one had a film to hand. we
have found out from a narrative in verse that he came from a deep dark

forest in order to look just once upon the rhine. and because he bore the lord's name on his tongue, they hung him upside down. and when the peasant found him in the thornbush they say there was a light shining

all around him and the sick were healed by it. so did he come up from the cellar or didn't he. so much for the chronicler's report. like someone coming home from war, into his village; a film-maker; the way he looks at the slightly

yellowed landscape. the slope; the gallows hill, across which the wind blows. and the way a man stands there, in a smithy, hardly looking up; the way he strikes the iron, until sparks fly. and this time there is a film in the camera.

underground

oval, clapham, edgware road .. so this is how they lived in the underground, in the blitz, escalators, rubber, stench in the nights, announcements meant for everyone: *mind the gap* .. the stream

of people carrying me along and along, on through the tunnels, through all tunnels, tunnels of concrete covered in images, how far can you go without getting hungry. escalators, endless,

up to the air. stood there and climbed and read while standing. among people, inflammable as I was, two eyes led down the shaft. in the uncertain hour before the morning, near the ending of

interminable night over the asphalt where no other sound was between three districts whence the smoke arose .. smoke .. this is where they brought the dead, their ashes, stardust, into the

innermost, the chamber. where the light reached in the longest night. on the winter island. in the chamber, high and narrow. loose stones, tightly layered, no need for mortar, no concrete.

and the spirals, circles, that they scored in the massive stone they carted here through all the land, through space and time: the pure order they clearly possess can surely not be anything

as chaotic as writing. so I stood there and read while standing. not ornament, not mere decoration. the original image, the sun, crossed the landscape with tumuli through which the boyne

goes on its way, the lightning, the blitz, descended, the blitz came and accepted the sacrifice. what they scratched there was abstraction .. then they came to erect the high cross and chiselled

figures from the sandstone. there they are standing at its two
sides: rising here, falling there. *mind the gap*. they laid the dead
in the earth, intact, in his image, to wait for him until he should

come again. the blitz came over the landscape. they carted
stones to build the tunnels; the blitz came over the landscape:
what were they after in the underground—disturbing the peace

of the dead? smell of rubber and I climbed and climbed .. day
was breaking, and the fresh air lifted my spirits a little in a kind
of valediction and I faded on the blowing of the all clear horn

tobernalt

drive more slowly, the road is already rolling down
to the lake as described. there is the sign and under
this tree is the place where the flock used to meet in
secret as soon as word went round that the shepherd
was on his way. he had spent the night out in the
open somewhere here in ireland in the penal times.
the one they were waiting for came on foot carrying in a
sack the things that were needed: chalice and sacrificial
bowl, carefully wrapped in a white cloth, and carrying with
special care the monstrance. the bread, untransformed,
came in the ciborium. but the water was already here, here
at the source, in which I'll at least have to bathe my feet ..
look more slowly, there is the stone altar and up there is
the grotto from which mary looked down on them all as
they did their rounds on their knees of the stations and
mysteries: where patrick came with his clover leaf to teach
the celts about the trinity. it says so here. scabs on their
knees, their hands covered in mud, their eyes sought
something in the sky in which I can see clouds like sheep.
the thing itself didn't take long: they rattled off the liturgy
as always, but for a good hour all heaviness was lifted
from them .. think more slowly, things are occurring to me:
the marks were not only on their hands, but what could not
be washed off again with *ata* could be spoken through the
screen; they'd be absolved and then they were pure. but I
scratched the scabs on my knees again until they bled and
then new dirt got in. take another picture of me with bare
feet. help me put my shoes back on, I can hear them coming.

primrose street

the parking space fitted precisely and a little while later
I was standing at the door of a small house and knocking
knocking until it opened stood straight away in the *sitting
room* with voices drawing together around me from the
unfamiliar tongues of *mums* and *babies* and I was certain
that it must be irish. the carpet was strewn with leaves
and needles from trees of strange species while *leprechauns*
danced before me in the toy forest there was a light on
the video channel in the tunnel that led deep down into
their mountain world there were *fairies* dancing there
with short-styled hair maybe they were singing but I
could not understand very much just sometimes it sounded
like *how are you?* and I was certain that it must be irish.
I was imprisoned in a mountain of dull sound. there were
passages there where the smell of tea was drifting but
no-one offered me a cup. no it was more acrid was
the smell of tar it was violence was pressure of pneumatic
hammers working outside and drilling into the mountain
images were flashing through my mind. there was a *dad*
sitting in a little kitchen surrounded by *mums* who was
talking on and on and I was certain that it must be irish.
I held my tongue so that no-one would see me stretched
out my hand towards the brightly coloured treasures
that the *leprechauns* were bearing past me but it was
only air and everything was going through my head
police cars or *mobile phones* with colourful buttons
and distorted voices. I was a cave and fitted precisely:
I was imprisoned in a mountain of dull sound.

crossing

the wind is working among the chestnut trees. I used to walk along this avenue as a child: it's blocked off now because of the danger of branches breaking off. it led from the monastery to schloss dyck via the dyck wine house in damm the way led back to the monastery. inside is dark and cool as always. I dip my hand into the font cross myself in the nave I see the brass plates in the floor with the names of the von salm-reifferscheidt family. in the wall an epitaph (marble). the person resting here was once a count: the first death's head I saw in my life. the bones jutting out from the relief like the vein in father's temple when he was laid low with one of his headaches I was asked to massage him the vein pulsing my fingers stroking his hot brow, along the cold stone. two tablet halves daily he always took me with him on his walks to the water but there was no barque, no ferryman, no styx in the monastery garden the jüchener stream marked the boundary between cologne and aachen. we'd be across it in a single step.

pan's hour

etching

the wide mountain landscape with four trees that an old
etching shows reminds me of something from my dreams
when only an image remains on waking I know I was walking

through a wide-open region that gave me the impression
that I'd been there before but all the paths ran differently
so that I saw no other person ever or it was the hilly

landscape with a tower that stands on the floor of the valley
to the right and to the left the gigantic battered tree-crown
waving against a bright and empty sky .. then there were

boulders on the ground and everything was dark again and
soon the word moraine occurred to me and rocks were standing
there like in the desert and even the trees were petrified I was

driven and I was lost as long as nothing came along the path
I heard someone crying and could feel my bones I turned around
and saw that my light was still on and that I was lying there alone

early spring

my child has been ill. for just one night she's lain there in a fever.
now she sees violets where none are growing yet. the spring
storms are still here and in the yard the wind is howling round

the bins. strange things in her fevered imaginings .. my daughter
orders me to stoop down to the flowers, but does not know about
my back and that we're shut in. we listen to the radio and play

cards. the magpie on the roof. my daughter wins. now I have to sit
still while my daughter sings a song. she wants me to be somebody
else and I would be glad to be for nothing's going right for me today.

then we watch tv for an hour .. and once upon a time I myself was
standing in the garden. there was a laburnum, it was may, in a photo
I look apprehensive .. then we look at the moon and the evening

star. we sit beneath an elder bush and wait. would that the swifts would
come and chase each other swooping up to our eaves; then something
that's been oppressing me may lift and then I'd wave, and then I'd wave.

indian summer

summer was resurgent the forecast for friday being
even warmer we thought we'd drive out into the country
you had still not quite recovered. I'd gauged the end

of the traffic jam and so we left earlier than planned (the
load on the back of a lorry was in flames) to try our luck
in country lanes. briefly uneasiness overcame me when

I couldn't find the road in question and signs were pointing
us in *all directions*. at last glancing at your watch you said let's
go back to that place we found that time some months ago.

the spot seemed much the same. but the fruit on the trees
had already been ripening for quite a while you picked us some
plums they were floury already and their taste was almost gone.

it was just like last time at the same hour. the water mirrored the
high light and we tried to walk around the lake but this time we
could not manage the whole way quite. we sat by the weir in the tall

reeds where the other shore was out of sight and something was
tickling at your legs and so we could not stay for very long. stinging
nettles were stinging. then on the way back you fell asleep. I looked

alone at the unpeopled land. how straight the roads here ran through
pines and sand. how early the lights went on. I looked silently at your
blonde lashes and gripped the steering wheel firmly in my hand.

german autumn

dark clouds hang over the elbe valley. the lilienstein is
shrouded in dense mist. we weren't here when the rivers
overflowed, but the dampness comes and gets into

our bones and this mark on the wall shows how high the
water was on the sixteenth of august. you say you're cold
and want to go on ahead back to the car, and can I bring

you your thick socks when I go back to our room. this
summer we talked about how dark it can be in german
towns, whether it's bacharach, bad sulza or here in königstein.

if the days are overcast and dismal then as well, there's just
the food left to cheer us up, for a short time. the heating
roars and then we have to air and from the room with the

antlers on the wall, the coal stove and the panelling the voice
of herr zimmermann from vienna comes up through the floor.
he's been coming here for years, he travels alone and entertains

us all. we lie under heavy feather duvets and we pray that this
night may pass us by. I do not want to feel the crack between
our mattresses. then a toilet flushes. it's only half past one.

pan's hour

when we found a space to park by the shop to buy some water
and didn't like the look of the place I remembered what my parents
used to say: I wouldn't want to have my picture taken here.

we set off across the field you were carrying your camera over
your shoulder and when you stopped at the edge of the woods to
adjust the settings I noticed the shimmer of your light-sensitive skin

as the path wound through the trees the land descended sooner
than we'd expected the *kossenblatter see* was below us reflecting
back the midday light that was slanting on to it. I mentioned this

and sought your eyes we practised the ancient art of renaming
the things around us on the landing stage the heron stayed
still for just long enough the buzzard was above us beneath the

sky we walked quickly without stopping both determining the
brimstone butterfly and for more than an hour we were simply
there in an hour where neither you nor I had ever been before.

syrinx

a hot breath on my neck that woke me: you slid your
tongue into my ear I was already dreaming when you lay
down beside me so freshly showered and wearing no pyjamas.

then we lay there staring at the ceiling. you let me hear
your silent reproach. all I said was that I would not say
anything else just now. then we spoke and only stumbled

even more. the darkness I go into is complete. even the trams
outside are empty at this hour. only my footsteps on the
pavement echoing. the first light emerging from the

bakeries. the first birds waking up. perhaps you are
sleeping. but I'm the coldest of all and cannot forgive
myself. all that redeems me is the hotness of your breath.

fire

the train was late. a cutting was on fire. a spark's enough
in these conditions: the fire caught hold of the bone-dry grass
growing everywhere between the tracks, and spread to the
dessicated broom. ticks were roasting in the broom. in the thick
smoke through the window I could hardly see the monorail
moving through the mist. now we must have crossed the wupper.
I saw and sensed something at the edge of vision. two old
women, snow-white hair and a stony stare: we recognise you
and you are cursed. we can kill without touching. I sat stiff
as a poker and did not turn around. changed trains in cologne
and took the quieter line. in the restaurant car the food stayed cold.
I pressed my skull against the window staring as though petrified
out into the dusk. a woman with a perm with streaks of grey
snapped her handbag open and spoke to me in a sing-song
rhineland voice, whereupon I recognised her from the way
she snapped her chocolate. she could only stay an hour. we
shared a final bar. she blessed me quickly. then she shut her bag.
she had to leave me in coblenz. it was june, and everywhere
outside the cuttings were on fire, the poppies in full bloom.

the year of the soul

I left yet another message on her machine in cologne and
wondered if she was standing there listening to my voice
without picking up. possible that she couldn't find the phone
straight away or that the children were practising the piano
fortissimo or that the spaghetti water was boiling over. in
fact I almost preferred it that way. I'm sure she must still
have been busy packing. we didn't usually talk for very
long on the phone unlike when I'd be sitting in the armchair
eating things from the garden and she'd pour me more tea
and pass me freshly-baked cake. what we'd talk about then
was mostly the same. we don't hear anything from various
friends any more and that thing with berit was a long time ago
as well and how we'd meet in the hohenzollernring back when
we would be living for ever .. until we got to talking about
stifter and I'd take another piece of cake and we'd read poems
from *the year of the soul* .. the years went by with no variation
and each of us thought the others would still be there and that
the tea would stay for ever on the warmer. what will happen
now to all her furniture that came from her grandmother's
house what will become of the heavy old oak furniture.

ferns

I'd left my watch again, but it must have been around
midday as we walked for the second time along the
path to zühlsdorf. a friend had come with us we talked

about things of the present and the way the light fell
almost vertically among the trees brush and undergrowth
were glowing and stumps revealed their age-rings. we

walked along like this and had no sense of distance and
soon we reached a place I still remembered from the first
occasion. a white butterfly flew up ahead of us into the

brightness and suddenly there was the fire lane. the iron
pylons carrying current overland were standing there as they
always had and high above us the wires shimmered coming

to and going from we knew not where. we stood in the
undiminished light. heather was in bloom. shards of pots
were in the path you put a blue one in your pocket. I looked

over to the young fir trees and each of us was on our own for
a moment. images from earlier blended in I do not know what
level of memory engendered them and as we went back into the

dark I saw the question in your eyes. then we continued the
conversation. it was still pleasantly warm. we continued on
our way to zühlsdorf. ferns were growing along the path.

Author's Notes

from far away (p. 23)—Lines in italics refer to the first stanza of Hölderlin's hymn 'Der Rhein': "Im dunkeln Epheu ... so vernahm ich ohne Vermuthen .. sich manches beredend".

winter journey (p. 24)—Contains various quotes from and allusions to German Romantic tradition. The main reference is to the cycles *Winterreise* and *Die schöne Müllerin* by Wilhelm Müller (1794–1827), set to music by Franz Schubert (1797–1828).

against the light (p. 34)—"beneath the bushes sat an earnest bird songless" refers to Hölderlin's elegy 'Der Wanderer': "Unter dem Strauche saß ein ernster Vogel gesanglos." The bird's speech in my poem recalls the stranger's monologue in Eliot's 'Little Gidding II'.

fruit (p. 37)—"At the still point of the turning world": cf. Eliot, 'Burnt Norton IV'.
—Andreas Baader (1943–77) was the leader of the first generation of German terrorists known as "RAF" (*Rote Armee Fraktion*). During his imprisonment in Stuttgart-Stammheim (where he was found dead in the aftermath of the Schleyer abduction) his conditions of detention were a frequent topic in German papers. I remember especially one headline which announced that he was allowed to play table tennis. "I read the Bader catalogue" is a pun making use of the homophone mail order catalogue. From around the same time, I remember listening to news of the Vietnam War and the battle of Hué which was referred to as "die alte Kaiserstadt"—a title that could also refer to Aachen, where the German emperors used to be crowned.
—"regular issue chocolate bar": I think of the chocolate bars that were part of the *Einmannpaket*, a soldier's food supplies during the Second World War.—"faded sütterlin": From 1935–1941, Sütterlin script was taught in German schools.

dürer's young venetian girl (p. 50)—Over the years, I have written quite a few poems about my grandmother's small flat which was a magic place in my childhood. All the walls were covered with calendars and paintings, mostly landscapes, and all of them prints, not originals, but the child that used to look at them did not care about that.

the song of the black letter (p. 52) is all about my memories of reading Edgar Rice Burroughs' *Tarzan* novel when I was a boy. The way Tarzan learned to read just by gazing at the letters in the books he found in the jungle without being taught by anyone fascinated me.

traces (p. 54)—In 2001, I read an article about zebra finches and their newly discovered ability to listen to the song of their species even in sleep. In 1986, I dreamed of the *Challenger* space shuttle crash, and I have come to think that I may have had this dream *before* the crash happened. So the poem is about our ways of obtaining knowledge, and the question which interests me is whether the knowledge we get by technical means of the most developed kinds is really more accurate than the knowledge we obtain in dreams.—The *eliot cassettes* feature the poet's voice reading 'The Waste Land', 'Four Quartets' and other poems.

silent sources (p. 58)—"Then he fell for the third time" alludes, of course, to the passion of Christ. My private thoughts, though, go to my uncle who managed to have a heart attack three times in the same church (where he was part of the choir) over the years, until he finally died there.

dance of death (p. 64)— 'Fear of the Dark' and 'Dance of Death' are the title tracks of two albums by the British heavy metal band, Iron Maiden.

berlin fresco (p. 65)—In 1860, during restoration works in the tower hall of St. Mary's Church in Berlin (near Alexanderplatz), a giant fresco dating from the 15th century was discovered by the royal chief architect, August Stüler. It shows a 22-metre-long dance of death with rhymed verses beneath it, depicting in graphic detail how all classes in medieval society are called alike by the grim reaper.

september light (p. 71)—Konrad Adenauer (1876–1967), former mayor of Cologne and then first chancellor of the Federal Republic of Germany, used to spend his holidays in Cadenabbia on Lake Como in his late years. His former villa now hosts a guest house run by the Adenauer Foundation, and once a year, there is a writer's workshop. Adenauer was famous for his small vocabulary and Rhenish accent, but also feared for his wit and irony. Rhöndorf is a village close to Bonn where he lived after he was expelled from Cologne by the Nazis. On his way to the Bundestag, he used the ferry at Mehlem where crowds of followers welcomed him after victorious elections.

calendar (p. 75)—The ARD is the German equivalent to the BBC.

all hallows (p. 77) is the day when Catholics in the Rhineland go to visit their family graves, which are specially spruced up in the days leading up to it. I wrote this poem when I was about to leave the Rhineland and go to Berlin, where these Catholic traditions are hardly known.

legend (p. 78) refers to the medieval Rhenish Werner myth. A 15-year-old lad from the woodlands and servant in a house at Oberwesel, Werner was found dead on Good Friday 1287, and the local Jews were accused of having committed a ritual murder. This caused great hysteria, and 40 Jewish people were killed by the infuriated mob. Werner was canonised, and his chapel can still be visited at Bacharach. The final lines of the poem, however, fuse his legend with scenes from Edgar Reitz' *Heimat*, a highly-acclaimed epic on German television and abroad. *Heimat* focuses on the Hunsrück area, where Werner came from.

underground (p. 80) contains several quotations from and allusions to Eliot's 'Little Gidding II': "In the uncertain hour before the morning . . . and faded on the blowing of the horn". In the German, these quotes are given in my own translation of Eliot's 'Four Quartets'. The poem was written shortly after the terrorist attacks on London Underground in July 2005. Around this time I was in Ireland and visited the passage tomb at Newgrange in Co. Meath, on the river Boyne, and also several Celtic crosses. Impressions of an article about the history of the London Underground—possibly from *The Guardian*—and some frightening pictures from the remake of *War of the Worlds* (feat. Tom Cruise) that I saw in a Dublin cinema were also buried in my underground poem.

tobernalt (p. 82) is a holy well at Lough Gill, Co. Sligo, Ireland.

crossing (p. 84)—The monastery is the *Nikolauskloster* close to Neuss, the place where I was born.

etching (p. 87)—Refers to several etchings by the Dutch artist Hercules Seghers (1590–1638).

pan's hour (p. 91)— Kossenblatter See is a lake near Görsdorf, in a thinly populated area of rural Brandenburg. It is revisited in *indian summer. (p. 89)*.

the year of the soul (p. 94)—In 1897, German symbolist poet Stefan George (1868–1933) published *Das Jahr der Seele* which became his best known volume of poems. These poems have a remarkable impact when read aloud. Adalbert Stifter (1804–1868): Austrian novelist. One of his greatest works is *Der Nachsommer*.

ferns (p. 95)—Zühlsdorf is a small village north of Berlin, near Oranienburg.

syrinx (p. 92)—Syrinx is a nymph who ran away from the Greek god Pan who wanted to make love to her. She was transformed into a reed, from which Pan carved his flute.

fire (p. 93)—"We can kill without touching" alludes to a line by Hugo von Hofmannsthal (1874–1929) from his poem 'Der Prophet', about his encounter with Stefan George: "Und er kann töten ohne zu berühren."

I wish to dedicate this selection of my poems to my wife, Nadja Küchenmeister.